BREEDERS' BEST®

A KENNEL CLUB BOOK

Doberman Pinscher

By Victor Clemente

BREEDERS' BEST™
A KENNEL CLUB BOOK®

DOBERMAN PINSCHER

ISBN: 1-59378-929-7

Copyright © 2004

Kennel Club Books, LLC
308 Main Street, Allenhurst, NJ 07711 USA
Printed in South Korea

PHOTOS BY:
Paulette Braun,
Isabelle Français,
Carol Ann Johnson
and Bernd Brinkmann.

DRAWINGS BY:
Yolyanko el Habanero

Contents

Meet the Doberman Pinscher

The Doberman Pinscher, one of the most popular dogs in America, indeed the world, appears elegant of form, powerfully built, medium in size and ever so sharp. This is a breed that is smart and quick to learn, and needs an owner who is also smart and willing to train his dog. Before purchasing a Doberman, you would be wise to do a bit of reading about the breed, attend a dog show or two and talk to responsible breeders.

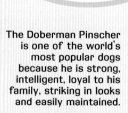

The Doberman Pinscher is one of the world's most popular dogs because he is strong, intelligent, loyal to his family, striking in looks and easily maintained.

The history of the Doberman Pinscher is a "short" history compared to those of many other breeds. The Rottweiler, another handsome black and tan German breed, can trace its roots back to Caesar and Roman times; some of the running hounds go back to early Egyptian times and many Toy breeds boast of their ancestors' being captured by the Renaissance masters! The Doberman owes his being to Herr Frederick Louis Dobermann, born in Apolda, Thuringa, Germany in 1834.

The Doberman was originally bred as a working guard dog. Today many families appreciate their Dobermans' instincts for protecting home and family.

Herr Dobermann had numerous occupations, including night-watchman, policeman, tax collector and dog catcher. As he watched over the numerous and varied dogs that passed through the pound, he thought that he could develop a new breed of dog that could protect him as he worked at his various duties. Herr Dobermann worked diligently toward his goal of developing a new breed but,

All dogs likely derived from a common ancestor, *Canis lupus*, the gray wolf.

unfortunately, he did not keep records of which dogs were bred, nor do we know why a particular dog was selected to be added to the breeding program.

The likely breeds that were used to develop the "brainchild" of Herr Dobermann probably started with the German Pinscher, a medium-sized terrier and guard-dog breed. Other breeds that certainly were pertinent to the development of the Doberman Pinscher, as we know it today, are the Rottweiler and the

The preference for the breed in the US is cropped ears and a docked tail.

A Doberman from the breed's homeland, Germany. Notice the uncropped ears and natural long tail.

Manchester Terrier (then known as the Old Black and Tan). Possibly, the Great Dane and the Greyhound also played a part in the creation of the breed.

In the breed's homeland, it is known simply as the Dobermann, a name that applies to all of Europe, including the United Kingdom. Americans refer to the breed as the Doberman Pinscher, omitting the second "n" in the founder's name and adding the German word *pinscher*, which means "biter."

After the death of Herr Dobermann, several other individuals in Germany became active in the breed, notably Goswin Tischler, who produced the first Dobermann champion, and Otto Goeller, who established the first breed club, the Dobermannpinscher Klub. By 1900, the breed received official recognition and the Dobermann standard was accepted by the German Kennel Club.

The breed gained in popularity throughout the world, with Doberman Pinschers showing up in Europe and, shortly after, in America. The first Doberman was imported to the United States in 1898, and the first Doberman was registered in the American Kennel Club (AKC) Stud Book in 1908. This was Doberman Intelectus, a German import. Intelectus became the first AKC Doberman champion. In the same year, Theodore Jager opened his Doberman Kennels and the first American-bred Doberman, Doberman Dix, came from this kennel.

With the advent of World War I, the breed came upon hard times in Europe. Many of the dogs were recruited into the military and those that weren't came upon the same food shortages that the human population faced.

The Doberman is a versatile canine companion, capable of participating in activities with his owner or just being man's— or woman's— best friend!

Breeders sent their dogs to the US, where they would have the proper care and attention rather than being lost through lack of food. After the war, the breed's popularity grew throughout the world, with excellent dogs being bred in the US as well as the breed's making a strong recovery in Germany.

In America, Carlo of Rhinegold, bred by F. F. H. Fleitman of Westphalia Kennels, was the first American-bred Best in Show winner. By 1939, Sieger Ferry von Rauhfelsen, owned by Mrs. Geraldine Dodge of Giralda Farms, was the first Doberman to win Best in Show at the Westminster Kennel Club dog show, the most famous show in the US.

The official breed club, the Doberman Pinscher Club of America, was founded in 1921 and the breed continued to gain popularity throughout the world.

During the 1920s, the American breeders bred for a more elegant dog, with an arched neck replacing the short neck, and the light eye becoming darker and clear. The coat colors, rather than just black and tan, expanded to black, red, blue and fawn. Through time, the Doberman has become a sleek, sophisticated and aristocratic dog, much admired by members of the working-dog set and the show-dog set alike. Today, the breed is counted among the most popular breeds in the US and in Great Britain. The breed competes successfully in conformation as well as obedience and agility trials.

The athletic Dobe makes agility look easy. Look at this dog navigate the weave poles with precision and grace.

The Doberman Pinscher, a member of the American Kennel Club's Working Group, is a highly desirable guard dog due to his intelligence and quick learning abilities. He has a keen nose for tracking and can fulfill his duties as a sentry with ease, making him a sought-after watchdog for homes and businesses. With all of these abilities, he has also become a great friend and companion dog to those who understand his temperament and can provide the proper home and training.

The Doberman's sleek coat looks magnificent in any color. This dog's rich red coat simply shines.

MEET THE DOBERMAN PINSCHER

Overview

- The Doberman Pinscher was developed in Germany by Herr Frederick Louis Dobermann.
- The breed is known as the Dobermann in Europe.
- American breeders refined the breed's elegance. Its intelligence and sleek looks have made it one of the most popular breeds worldwide.
- The Doberman's many talents and trainability have enabled him to perform in various capacities, including messenger and war dog, a show dog, competition dog and guardian.

Description of the Doberman

Every breed of dog registered with the American Kennel Club has a breed standard, and this standard gives a mental picture of what the breed should look and act like. The Doberman Pinscher is a working breed and thus is classified in the Working Group of dogs. Working dogs are known for their abilities, which include guarding and protecting, pulling a cart or sled or rescuing a drowning person. The Doberman is considered

The Doberman Pinscher has often found itself employed by the military for various duties, including search-and-rescue during wartime.

a guard or sentry dog, and a well-bred Doberman will carry through with his duties in a supreme manner.

In general appearance, the Doberman is a medium-sized, square dog with a compact, muscular body built for great endurance. The standard states that he is "Elegant in appearance, of proud carriage, reflecting great nobility and temperament. Energetic, watchful, determined, alert, fearless, loyal and obedient." The males weigh between 75 and 90 pounds and the females are a bit smaller, at 55 to 70 pounds. They are approximately 26 to 28 inches high at the shoulder.

The Doberman presents a sleek outline, accentuated by his musculature and close coat. This is a typical American dog with cropped ears and docked tail, seen in the popular black and tan coloration.

The Doberman is a sleek-coated breed. The new owner must be aware that this is a dog that will not be able to live outdoors, as he cannot tolerate either great heat or cold. This will be an indoor dog for you! The advantage of the short coat, however, is that grooming will be at a minimum. He

A Doberman whose ears have not been cropped and taped to stand upright will have natural drop ears.

lives for approximately ten years, but there are health problems in the breed of which you should be well aware when purchasing your first Doberman. Responsible breeders continually work on breeding out any genetic problems.

The Doberman is a high-energy breed. All new owners have to be aware that this is a breed that will require early and consistent training from their owners. This is a dog that must know very early on who the boss is in the household. If he feels that you are not the superior being, he will, with his great intellect, quickly take over and become the ruler of the household. You must not let this happen, but with early and consistent training you have a running start.

He likes to be with his family, doing things in the great outdoors. While he may be content to sit by your side while you read the newspaper, he wants to "go go go" and wants his owner by his side. He likes to go for walks, hikes and car rides, and he will want to chase a ball or catch a Frisbee. He wants attention and he needs to know that he is a part of the family. If you work long hours, he will not do well by himself, confined to a crate or a room. This can be an open invitation for him to become destructive and to cause trouble that you can do without.

In addition to being a companion for the family, he will also be a guard dog, offering you, your family and your property protection, as this is what he has been bred for. This is a powerful dog with large jaws and teeth, a dog who will stand his ground against anything that he thinks is threatening to his family. Some insurance companies list him as a "dangerous dog" and will not insure a household that owns a Doberman. Find out about this before purchasing a Doberman, or, better yet, choose a less ignorant insurance company!

Dobermans are also very versatile and, because of their great intellect and easy train-ability, they can do very well in sports like agility and obedience, as well as search-and-rescue and other activities that require a good sense of smell. The Doberman has a handsome long nose that gives him considerable olfactory superiority—use his nose for good!

The Doberman is well known for his performance in times of war. During World War I, Germany had several thousand dogs in the military service, including German Shepherds and Dobermans. Before long, the United States and England were also training dogs for military service. During World War II, it is estimated that the US military services had over a

There are special training programs to prepare Dobermans for police duties. Sleeve training, as shown here, is also a component of Schutzhund work, a traditional German training discipline for protection dogs.

quarter of a million dogs commissioned for service, and many of these were Dobermans. The US Marines even gave the Doberman the designation of Marine War Dog. It is written that of all the breeds selected for military service (and even a few Sealyham Terriers were put to work), only the Doberman excelled in every area of performance, which included detecting mines, assaulting the enemy, guarding prisoners and many other jobs.

The breed standard, the written description of what the perfect breed member

White Dobermans are ineligible for showing and should never be bred, as they are not as genetically sound as normal-colored representatives of the breed.

looks and acts like, is very specific in describing the temperament of the breed: "Energetic, watchful, determined, alert, fearless, loyal and obedient. The judge shall dismiss from the ring any shy or vicious Doberman." A shy dog is determined by his shrinking away from the judge, refusing to stand for examination or shying away from unusual sounds. A vicious dog is described as one who has a belligerent attitude toward other dogs or who attempts to bite either the judge or his handler.

The acceptable colors for the Doberman are black, red,

blue and fawn, the latter of which is also called Isabella. There is also a "white" Doberman called the "albino" Doberman. This is not an acceptable color and dogs of this color should not be bred, as they carry many traits that are not acceptable to the Doberman's health or temperament. Do not let any individual sell you a Doberman of this color by telling you that this is a "rare" Doberman or one that is more valuable than a Doberman of a recognized color. This is not a respon-sible breeder and this is a dog that you should not buy. Find yourself a responsible breeder and buy a dog of one of the acceptable colors.

There are many reasons why a prospective owner would want to own this breed. A well-bred Doberman can be a joy to have as a pet. He can be an extremely affec-tionate companion and he is very trainable with his high degree of intellect, making a versatile dog to participate in a range of activities with his owner.

DESCRIPTION OF THE DOBERMAN

Overview

- The breed standard, devised by the parent club, describes the ideal Doberman, detailing physical conformation as well as character and movement.
- The Doberman's body should appear compact, square and muscular, "elegant in appearance, of proud carriage."
- The Doberman's ears and tail are typically cropped in the US; in Europe, these modifications are not made.
- The short-coated Doberman's recognized colors are black, red, blue and fawn. White or "albino" coloration is not acceptable.

Are You a Doberman Person?

The intelligent and intuitive Doberman makes a wonderful service dog for the handicapped. The breed is extremely well suited and used often for this type of work.

Before purchasing your Doberman Pinscher, you must give some thought to the personality and characteristics of this breed to determine if this is the right dog for you. This breed will not suit the laid-back owner who will not give the dog the daily exercise and attention that he requires, not to mention specialized training. The Doberman Pinscher, for all his regal bearing and superior intelligence, deserves to be owned and loved by an owner who understands the breed's unique characteristics, by a person who has studied up on the breed and who is willing and able to offer the dog the training and stimulation he needs to become the "super dog" that Herr Dobermann intended. Are you the right person to put the red cape on your superhero dog? You should answer the following questions before purchasing a Doberman:

If you think Greyhounds are fast, have a look at a Doberman in full flight!

1. Do you have the time to give to a dog? He will need care, companionship, training and grooming. This is almost like having a child, except that the dog remains a child and will always require your care and attention.

Time for a dog does not mean that you cannot work and own a dog. Your pet will need quality time, though, just like a child does. He must be fed two times a day and exercised several times a day. He

Despite the breed's reputation as fearless guard dogs, they are personable and affectionate. Some people might even call the breed "cuddly."

needs to be petted and loved, and he will like to go for rides in the car with you. You must work with him to have an obedient dog who has good manners. Your dog should have at least two good outings a day, and that means a walk or a good romp in the morning and the evening. Never let him out loose to run the neighborhood.

2. Do you have a fenced-in yard for your Doberman? This is not a breed that you can leave tied out on the porch or allow to run free. He must have a secure outdoor area in which

to run and exercise, with at least enough space for you to throw a ball and for your dog to run with it.

Remember, it is your responsibility to keep the yard clean of feces. When walking your dog, it is essential to carry a plastic bag or two to pick up droppings. These can be easily dropped in a handy trash receptacle on your way home.

3. Have you owned a dog previously, and did that dog live a long and happy life with your family? This will give you a good idea of what a dog expects from you and what

Who wouldn't feel safe with a pack of Doberman Pinschers on patrol?

you must do for your dog. In addition, the Doberman is smart and needs an owner that is equally as smart, or smarter, than he is!

4. Do you understand that your neighbors may not be pleased with your bringing this imposing breed into the neighborhood? You should talk to your neighbors about adding a Doberman to your household. Give them some information on the breed and reassure them that you are purchasing a temperamentally sound puppy from a responsible breeder and that you will give this dog the time, the care and the training that he will need.

5. Will you take the time to attend training classes and learn to train your dog to be an acceptable canine citizen? This is a breed that must be trained at an early age. Check out the obedience classes in your area, before bringing your puppy home, to see which type of training you prefer, as trainers vary in their training methods.

6. Do you have young children in the family? Are you expecting a baby in the near future? Young children when raised with a Doberman Pinscher are a winning combination. But if you are expecting a baby, you should

You must be able to take the time to train your Doberman while he is still a puppy in order to produce a reliable adult whose wonderful traits have been developed to the fullest.

think seriously about adding any dog to your family at this time of change in your lives.

7. Do you have the time and interest to care for this dog? Owning a dog is a full-time responsibility and the

Doberman requires more time for exercise and training than many other breeds. The breed thrives on time spent with his owner and will wither away if not offered daily stimulation, exercise and attention. Taking the dog to training classes or structuring a lesson plan for the dog at home, keeping up with the dog's veterinary visits, offering the dog fun outdoor activities and so on all require lots of time from the owner.

Even though the Doberman requires a minimum of grooming, he will require some coat care. Grooming is not extensive with this breed, but you will need to trim his toenails, brush him and wash his face once or twice a week, keep his ears clean and give him baths as needed.

In spite of the toughness of the dog and the occasional difficulty in acceptance of the breed by one's neighbors, the Doberman is appreciated for his intelligence and versatility, his devotion to his family, his abilities for guarding those around him and their possessions and his keen looks. However, do learn all you can

Training for agility provides the Doberman with much-needed physical and mental stimulation while strengthening the bond between dog and owner as the two of you learn together.

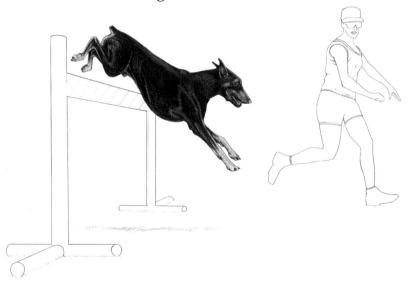

about the breed before rushing out and buying the first puppy you see.

For more information on the Doberman, check out other books on the breed and talk to the owners about their experiences. An excellent source of information can be found on the Internet by visiting the Doberman Pinscher Club of America— www.dpca.org. This website is a straightforward source of information from knowledgeable breed fanciers in addition to listing local Doberman clubs and breeders.

If you have the time to properly raise a Doberman, and you choose from a responsible breeder, you will be rewarded with a canine family member beyond compare. There's a reason why the breed is so well-loved the world over!

ARE YOU A DOBERMAN PERSON?

Overview

- The Doberman person is ready and able to assume a leadership role with the intelligent Doberman, who will be quick to take control if the owner does not establish himself as boss.
- The Doberman person has time to exercise and care for the dog and can provide ample accommodations.
- The Doberman person is responsible and committed to ensuring that his dog becomes a polite canine citizen. He is active and enjoys spending time with his dog.
- The Doberman person makes certain that his dog is safe at all times.

Selecting a Doberman Breeder

A litter of Dobe pups can be quite a handful! A dedicated breeder makes the welfare of his puppies a priority by making sure they all go to homes where they will receive the best care.

When you buy your Doberman Pinscher, you will want to buy a healthy puppy from a responsible breeder. A responsible breeder is someone who has given considerable thought before breeding his bitch. He considers health problems in the breed, has screened his sire and dam for hip dysplasia and other known congenital diseases, has room in his home or kennel for a litter of puppies and has the time to give to a litter. He does not breed to the dog down the block because it is easy or to show his children what the miracle of birth is all about.

A responsible breeder is someone who is dedicated to the breed and to breeding out any faults or hereditary problems, and whose overall interest is in improving the breed. He will study pedigrees and see what the leading stud dogs are producing. To find the right stud dog for his bitch, he may fly his bitch across the country to breed to a particular stud dog, or he may drive the bitch to a dog who is located a considerable distance away. He may only have one or two litters each year, which means that there may not be a puppy ready for you when you first call. Remember that you are purchasing a new family member and that usually the wait will be well worth it.

Check out the Doberman Club of America's website (www.dpca.com)

All pups in the litter should be clean, healthy-looking and brimming with personality.

A handsome youngster, well on his way toward a bright future.

for listings of and links to regional breed clubs. You should be able to find one in your state, or at least in your region, as there are many clubs. The local club should be able to find a responsible breeder for you, and he should be able to answer any questions that you may have.

The responsible Doberman breeder will probably be someone who has been breeding for some years and someone who is known on the national level. He will be a member of the local Doberman club and will also belong to the Doberman Pinscher Club of America. The responsible breeder will show you his kennel, if there is one, or invite you into his home to see the puppies. The areas will look and smell clean. The breeder will show you the dam of the litter that you are looking at, and she will be clean, smell good

and be friendly. All of the puppies will also be healthy and clean, with trimmed toenails and clean faces. He may only show you one or two puppies and, most likely, will not show you the puppies that are already sold or that he is going to keep.

The breeder will also have questions for you, a whole battery of questions. Be prepared to answer any of the following questions, and have some questions of your own. Have you had a dog before? How many have you had and have you ever owned a Doberman? Did your dogs live a long life? Do you have a fenced yard? What are you intentions for the puppy? Showing, breeding, obedience, guard work, companion dog? How many children do you have and what are their ages? Are you willing to spend the time in teaching your children how to treat the

An uncropped four-and-a-half-month-old from Germany.

new family member? Have you ever done any dog training and are you willing to go to obedience classes with your dog? Are there any other pets in your household?

Do not be offended by

Now it's your turn to "interrogate" the breeder. You will be spending ten or more years of your life with this dog, so there's no reason—absolutely none— to be hasty. Know what to look for and be prepared to keep looking until you find

When visiting the breeder, you will meet the dam and her lovely litter of puppies. The dam should be protective of her brood though not act aggressively or nervously with her visitors.

these questions. The breeder has put a lot of time, effort and money into his litter and his first priority is to place each pup in a caring and appropriate household where the pup will be wanted, loved and cared for.

a breeder who answers your questions honestly and satisfactorily.

For your first visit to the kennel, leave home without your credit card and your checkbook. You are not going to buy the first puppy you meet, no matter how cute and perfect you think the blue or black pup is. To begin, ask to see the pedigree, which should include three to five generations of ancestry (parents, grandparents, etc.). Inquire about any titles in the pedigree, which might include "Ch." for Champion, "CD" for Companion Dog (an obedience trial title) or "SchH. I" (a Schutzhund title, a working title more frequently seen on European pedigrees). These titles and many others indicate a dog's accomplishments in some area of canine competition, which proves the merits of the litter's ancestors and adds to the breeder's credibility. While it is true that a pedigree is no guarantee of health or breed quality, it is still a good insurance policy.

You also will want to see the registration papers for the litter. The breeder should have registered the litter with the American Kennel Club (AKC). If the breeder tells you that the paperwork isn't "back yet" or that he doesn't register his dogs, you should not bother meeting the pups. Breeders do not charge you extra for registering the puppy. So, now you know.

Ask the breeder why he planned this litter. A good breeder should explain the genetics behind this particular breeding and what he expects the breeding to produce. The breeder who tells you that he breeds to raise funds to run his kennel should count on someone else's money, not yours! That is no reason to breed Dobermans, or any other dogs.

Ask to meet the sire and the dam of the puppies. The dam, most likely, will be available, though the sire may be owned by a different breeder, which is common. You should at least see photographs of the sire, hopefully standing in a show pose with a ribbon and a judge—not tied to a stake in a grassless backyard! The breeder should be able to introduce you to the dam as well as his other adult dogs, including some seniors or veterans (retired show dogs, etc.). It's a very positive sign to see that the breeder has a few generations of his breeding in his kennel.

By the way, if the breeder is producing multiple litters at one time, or has three or four (or more!) different breeds in his kennel, you are probably not visiting a dependable breeder. Some major kennels may offer several litters annually, but they are wealthy operations who are well equipped to properly raise and socialize their pups. You cannot mistake these reputable operations for backyard,

for-profit-only breeders. Some breeders even breed two breeds, such as Doberman Pinschers and Miniature Pinschers or Schnauzers, but if you meet a breeder who is breeding Dobes, Poodles, German Shepherds and Cockapoos, it's time to "hit the road." No breeder can responsibly know and breed more than two breeds at a time.

Ask the breeder about health clearances, as Dobermans can suffer from hip dysplasia, von Willebrand's disease and a number of other congenital problems. The sire and dam should have hip clearances from the OFA (Orthopedic Foundation for Animals, a national canine hip registry). Has the breeder had proper screening done on the sire and dam? Good breeders will gladly, in fact, proudly, provide those documents. For more information on genetic disorders

Doberman owners have to deal with after-care of cropped ears. Your breeder should give you complete instructions on how to clean the ears, how to change the tape, how often, for how long, etc.

in Dobes, you can check with the Doberman Pinscher Club of America's website.

Experienced breeders are frequently involved in some aspect of the dog fancy with their dog(s), perhaps showing them or training them for some type of performance event or dog-related activity. Their dogs may have earned titles in various canine competitions, which is added proof of their experience and commitment to the breed. If the breeder tells you that he doesn't go in for doggie beauty contests, or that the shows are all fixed or that he doesn't have time to breed and show, you should "move along, little doggie."

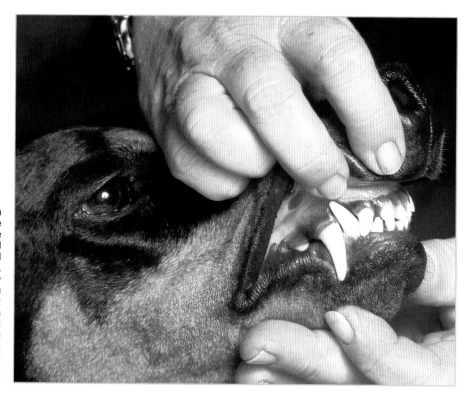

Strong teeth in a true scissors bite are required by the breed standard. A good breeder can help you predict how your pup's bite will develop as he matures. This is the typical bite of an adult.

The show ring is the proving ground for breeders, and dogs that cannot prove themselves in the show ring should never see the inside of a whelping box.

Dedicated breeders usually belong to the Doberman Pinscher Club of America and perhaps an area breed or kennel club. Such affiliation with other experienced breeders and sportsmen expands their knowledge of the breed and breed characteristics, which further enhances a breeder's credibility.

Surprise! These demonstrative Doberman puppies aren't afraid to show their breeder that they appreciate her attention and good care.

SELECTING A DOBERMAN BREEDER

Overview

- To find a reputable breeder, write, phone or email the American Kennel Club or the Doberman Pinscher Club of America for contacts.
- Visit a dog show to meet breeders and handlers of good dogs.
- Know what to expect from a quality breeder and be patient in your search.
- Ask about pedigrees, sales agreements, health clearances, registration papers and references.
- The breeder should inform you about the incidence of hip dysplasia, von Willebrand's disease and other hereditary conditions in his line.

Finding the Right Puppy

Y ou have passed the breeder's interrogation, and he has passed yours! You've decided that this breeder makes the grade and produces healthy, sound, typical Dobes. You are seeing eye-to-eye and you are now ready to select a puppy from an available litter. You will soon be a "Doberman person" and are ready to share your world with this big, courageous dog. You have checked out the local ordinances for dog-specific legislation and you have talked to your neighbors about bringing a Doberman onto your block.

How will you choose? Spend some time observing and interacting with the litter to see which pup's personality appeals to you most.

You arrive at the appointed time and the breeder has the puppies ready for you to meet and inspect. They should be a happy little pack, clean and alert. Their noses will be wet, their coats will have a glow or sheen and the pups will have a nice covering of flesh over their ribs, though will not be pot-bellied. Clear eyes indicate that the puppies are eating well and that they are clean and well cared for. Puppy coats may not glisten like those of adults, but they should not appear patchy or discolored. Use your common sense: Is this how you want your baby to look when visitors come to your home? If you are satisfied with the physical appearance of the pups, then you will be ready to pick up one of these rascals and cuddle him in your arms. Dobe pups should welcome visitors and be happy to meet you. Some may be more reluctant to be snatched up in your arms, but in time

Not all breeders will let their pups have a seat on the couch, but it's best when pups are raised in the home with the breeder's family rather than isolated in a kennel environment.

An ex-pen, soft padding and some toys make a nice area for the litter to spend some time outside their regular living quarters for some early socialization.

all the pups should warm up to your gestures and attention.

Find out from the breeder whether or not the sire and dam of the litter have had their temperaments tested. With a breed as powerful and intelligent as the Doberman, a temperament test is a very good idea. These tests are offered by the American Temperament Test Society (ATTS) and responsible breeders will be familiar with this organization and will have had their animals tested. The breeder will show you the score sheet and you can easily determine if the litter's parents have the personality you are looking for. In addition, this is another excellent indication that this is a responsible breeder.

Temperament testing by the ATTS is done on dogs that are at least 18 months of age; therefore, puppies are not tested, but the sire and dam of a litter can be tested. The test is like a simulated walk through a park or a neighborhood where everyday situations are encountered. Neutral, friendly and threatening situations are encountered to see what the dog's reactions are to the various stimuli. Problems that are looked for are unprovoked aggression, panic without recovery and strong avoidance. The dog's behavior toward strangers, reaction to auditory, visual and tactile stimuli and self-protective and aggressive behavior are watched. The dog is on a loose lead for the test and the test takes about ten minutes to complete. As of December 2002, the ATTS had tested 1,330 Dobermans, of which 1,011 passed. This is a 76% passing rate, which is slightly lower than in many breeds, making sound temperament a major concern in your choice of a pup.

Breeders will have the temperaments of their

Surveying his
territory is a
budding young
watchdog.

puppies tested by a professional, their veterinarian or another dog breeder. They will find the high-energy pup and the pup that is slower to respond. They will find the pup with the independent spirit and the one that wants to follow the pack. If the litter has been tested, the breeder will suggest which pup he thinks will be best for your family. If the litter has not been tested, you can do a few simple tests while you are sitting on the floor, playing with the pups.

Pat your leg or snap your finger and see which pup comes to you first. Clap your hands and see if one of the litter shies away from you. See how they play with one another. Watch for the one that has the appealing personality, as this will probably be the puppy that you will take home. Look for the puppy that appears to be "in the middle," not overly rambunctious, overly

aggressive or submissive. You want the joyful pup, not the wild or timid one.

Tell the breeder if you plan to show your pup in conformation or compete in performance-type events. Some pups will show more promise than others, and he can help you select one that will best suit your long-term goals. If you are considering a career in obedience for your Doberman, then a pedigree that shows obedience titlists will certainly be helpful. Follow the breeder's intuition about each puppy, as he has spent the last six to eight weeks with the litter and should have valuable insight.

Do you prefer a male or female? Both sexes are loving and loyal, and the differences are due to individual personalities rather than gender. Most hormone-related behavior issues are eliminated by spaying/neutering, which is beneficial for dogs not designated by the breeder

Every puppy is an individual. Few character traits hinge on the gender of the puppy.

as future show or breeding potential.

The Dobe female is a gentler soul and easier to live with but, like many females, she also can be a bit more moody, depending on her whims and hormonal peaks. She may also be a bit smaller, but both the male and female are fairly large animals.

In males, both testicles should be descended into the scrotum. A dog with undescended testicles will make a fine pet, but will be ineligible to compete in the show ring. The male tends to be more even-tempered than the bitch, and is also more physical and exuberant during adolescence, which can be problematic in a large and powerful dog. An untrained male can also become dominant with people and other dogs. A solid foundation in obedience

A puppy pose in front of the Christmas tree makes a nice photo, but it's never a good idea to surprise someone with a puppy for the holidays. Also, the hustle and bustle of the holidays can be quite a shock for a young pup who is trying to adjust to a new environment.

training is a prerequisite if you want your Dobe pup to respect you as his leader.

Spend some time selecting your puppy and, if you are hesitant, tell the breeder that you would like to go home and think over your decision. This is a major addition to your life, as you are adding a family member who may be with you for ten or more years. Be sure you get the puppy that you will all be happy with.

The serious quizzical expression of the puppy imparts the breed's intelligence even at a young age.

FINDING THE RIGHT PUPPY

Overview

- Arrange to visit the litter to meet the available pups. You are seeking a healthy, sound pup that has bright eyes, a shiny coat and a solid little frame.
- Ask if the parents have been temperament-tested and request to see the results.
- The breeder should be able to recommend a puppy that fits your home life and family.
- Decide upon a male or a female puppy based on certain personality and physical differences.
- If you intend to compete with the pup, discuss this with the breeder.
- Spend time with the puppies to see which pup best meets your selection criteria.

Welcoming the Doberman

So you have selected "Doberman puppy #6 with the yellow collar" from the litter and it's time to bring him home. Well, who would dream of leaving the maternity ward with "baby boy Smith" without naming him? It's time to name your puppy. Most owners and trainers believe that puppies respond best to two-syllable names, something rhythmic that ends in a vowel sound. For the Doberman, you might want to lean towards a Germanic name to reflect the breed's ancestry. You

Your puppy must be amenable to handling and cooperating with simple tasks like putting on his collar.

should avoid any "macho" names that can only cause problems for you and your dog in your neighborhood. You don't want to be bellowing, "Heel, Psycho, heel" as you're walking down the street, nor would it be comforting to your senior-citizen next-door neighbors to hear you scolding "Killer" every time he barks at a passing mail carrier. Once you have decided upon a good name for your Dobe, be prepared to use it frequently so that the puppy recognizes it.

Don't overwhelm little Henrik with too many toys all at once. Vary his toys from one play session to the next.

Name recognition is an important first step in training your puppy. You cannot underestimate the value of "Good, Henrik, good!" or "Atta girl, Eva!" Now let's welcome little Henrik or Eva into your home. But first....

Before welcoming your pup, you should buy food and water pans and a leash and collar. You should also purchase a crate for your puppy not only to sleep in but also to spend time in when he is home alone or

Bright eyes, moist nose, shiny coat and alert expression are signs of a healthy pup inside and out.

when you are otherwise unable to supervise. In very short order, your puppy will learn that the crate is his second "home," and he will feel safe and secure when he is in the crate. If the pup is left uncrated and alone, he will quickly become bored and begin to chew on things and snoop around, and could possibly get himself into

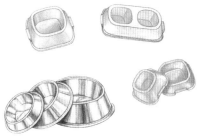

Select sturdy bowls for your Dobe, made of hard plastic or stainless steel.

danger. Keeping him in a confined area when you are away can eliminate these problems. And be sure to put several towels or a washable blanket in the crate so that he will be comfortable.

If you are driving some distance to pick up your pup, take along a towel or two, a water pan and your leash and collar. Also take along some plastic baggies and a roll of paper towels in case there are any potty accidents.

Before bringing your puppy into the house, you should be aware that a small puppy can be like a toddler and there are dangers in the household that should be eliminated. Electrical wires should be raised off the floor and hidden from view, as they are very tempting to chew. Swimming pools can be very dangerous, so make certain that your puppy can't get into, or fall into, the pool. Some barricades will be necessary to prevent an accident, as not all dogs can swim. Watch your deck railings and make sure that your puppy cannot slip through the openings and fall.

If you have young children in the house, you must ensure that they understand that the small puppy is a living being and

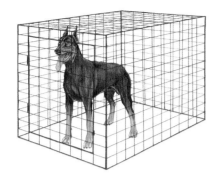

child, taught about animals at an early age, can become a lifelong compassionate animal lover and owner. Well-bred Doberman Pinschers living with responsible owners can make wonderful companions for children.

The wire crate is advantageous for use in the home, as it provides safe confinement while letting the dog feel a part of what's going on around him.

must be treated gently. They cannot ride on him or pull his ears, and he cannot be picked up and dropped. This is your responsibility. A

Use your common sense in all of the foregoing. Consider where a young child can get into trouble, and your puppy will be right behind

A Dobe-sized crate can fit a pack of pups, but each pup must be trained to individual crates once in their new homes. The crate must become a pup's place to call his own.

him! When the pup comes into the house for the first time (after he has relieved himself outside), let him look at his new home and surroundings, and give him a light meal and a pan of water. When he is tired, take him out again for a toilet trip and then tuck him into his crate, either to take a nap or, hopefully, to sleep through the night.

The first day or two for your puppy should be fairly quiet. He will then have time to get used to his new home, surroundings and family

Strong jaws and large teeth require only the sturdiest, most chew-resistant toys, designed specifically for large breeds. Your Dobe will always appreciate an interesting array of safe chew toys.

members. He may cry a bit during the first night, but if you put a teddy bear or a soft, woolly sweater in his crate, it will give him some warmth and security. A nearby ticking clock or a radio playing soft music can also be helpful. Remember, he has been uprooted from his siblings, his mother and his familiar breeder, and he will need a day or two to get used to his new family. If he should cry this first night, let him be and he will eventually quiet down and sleep. By the third night, he should be well settled in. Have patience and,

Children must respect dogs and treat them with kindness and care. The Dobe-and-child relationship can develop into a meaningful reciprocal friendship.

within a week or less, it will seem to you, your family and your puppy that you have all been together for years.

WELCOMING THE DOBERMAN

Overview

- Go to the pet store before your pup comes home! Puppy food, bowls, a collar and ID tags, toys, a leash, a crate and a brush are among the items you will need to have on hand.
- Make your home safe for your puppy by removing hazards from the dog's environment indoors and out.
- Let your pup become acclimated to his new surroundings, including taking him outdoors for toileting and introducing him to his crate.
- Introduce children to the puppy carefully and don't let your child hurt the pup. Make sure all family members treat the pup with care.

CHAPTER 7

House-training Your Doberman

Your dog must be housebroken, and this job should begin as soon as you bring him home. Diligence during the first two or three weeks will surely pay off and this should be a relatively easy task since the Doberman is so smart. Every time your puppy wakes up from a nap, he should be quickly taken outside. Watch him and praise him with "Good boy!" when he urinates or defecates. Give him a pat on the head and take him inside. He may have a few "accidents" indoors but with the appropriate "No" from you, he will quickly learn that it is better to go

An out-of-the-way site or your flowerbed? You choose where your Dobe's toilet area will be. Choose wisely, as he will always return to the same spot in the yard.

outside and do his "business" than to do it on the kitchen floor and be scolded.

You will soon learn your pup's habits. However, at the following times it is essential to take your dog out: when he gets up in the morning, after he eats, before bedtime and after long naps. Also monitor your pup's water intake to help predict his toilet needs. Most adult dogs will only have to go out three or four times a day. Some dogs will go to the door and bark when they want to be let out and others will nervously circle around. Watch and learn from your Dobe's signs. Of course, crates are a major help in housebreaking as most dogs will not want to dirty their living quarters.

Be patient with housebreaking, as this can sometimes be a trying time. It is simply essential to have a clean housedog. Life will be much easier for all of you—not to mention better for the carpeting!

Begin house-training as soon as your pup comes home. A fenced yard is ideal, as the pup will soon learn to locate his relief area on his own.

Be prepared to teach your Dobe clean toileting habits, one of the keys to a mutually happy coexistence with your dog.

Introduce the crate as soon as he comes home with a tasty cookie and a new command. Many owners simply say "Crate" or "Kennel" each time the puppy enters the crate. To instill a happy association with the crate, you can feed his first few meals inside the crate with the door open. Place the crate in a family room or some other room where the puppy will feel a part of his new pack. Here's the most important rule: Your puppy should sleep in his crate from his very first night. Don't start "tomorrow night"—you must begin right away. Despite his whining and scratching and sad eyes, be strong and do what's best for him and you (and your house). Whatever you do, do not take the puppy into bed with you. You'd be better off climbing in the crate with the puppy than having him "take over" your bed! During the day, place your puppy in his crate for naps, a little meal, chew-time with a special bone, and whenever you are unable to watch him closely. Fear not, your pup will let you

Male dogs lift their legs to urinate as a way of leaving their "calling card" for other dogs who pass by.

know when he needs "to go."

In order to housebreak the puppy, you must become the potty vigilante, keeping a close eye on the puppy all day. After he takes a drink, eats a meal or wakes up from napping, put on his leash and lead him outside to do his business. Now, let's teach another command "Outside" or "Hurry up." Use the command every time he "goes," lavishing him with praise. Use the same exit door for these potty trips, and lead him to the same spot. Watch for sniffing and circling or other signs that signal he has to relieve himself.

Don't be too hard on yourself or the puppy. All pups have accidents. If you catch him *in the act*, clap your hands and shout loudly— scoop him up to go outside. Your voice should startle him and make him stop. Be sure to praise when he finishes his duty outside. If you don't catch him, clean it up and scold *yourself* for not watching closely enough. Soon you'll have a reliable, clean housemate.

HOUSE-TRAINING YOUR DOBERMAN

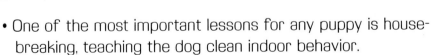

Overview

- One of the most important lessons for any puppy is house-breaking, teaching the dog clean indoor behavior.
- Using a crate to housebreak your puppy simplifies the process. Be consistent and watchful every hour of every day.
- Know when your puppy needs to go outside and always praise him when he "goes" where he should.
- Be patient and consistent. Never scold a puppy for piddling inside unless you catch him "mid-piddle."

Doberman Puppy Training

Your puppy should be well socialized when you bring him home. He will be used to meeting people, and average noises in the house and on the street will not startle him. Socialization for your puppy is very important and good breeders begin socialization early. If there were children in the breeder's family, the pup will be used to them as well. Let your dog meet the neighbors and play a few minutes. Take him for short walks in public places where he will see people and other dogs as well

Now's the time! Training a young pup results in the greatest success as you have the opportunity to teach him and instill good manners before he develops undesirable habits.

as hear strange noises. Watch other dogs, however, as they are not always friendly. Keep your dog on a short leash to keep control over him so he does not jump up on anyone.

You will find it to your advantage to have a mannerly dog; therefore, teaching your Dobe some basic commands will make your dog a better citizen. One of the family members should attend Puppy Kindergarten classes, which will teach good manners and serve as a basis for further training and activities. This is a class that accepts puppies from two to five months of age. It will take about two months to complete the class. You will cover the basics: sit, heel, down, stay and recall (come). There are definite advantages to each. Sit and heel are necessary when walking your dog. Who needs a puppy walking between your legs, lunging forward or lagging behind, in general acting like a nut? Teach your

Training results in good dog-owner communication, as the dog learns to understand and respond to your verbal commands and hand signals, and you learn to interpret his body language.

Pretty as a picture! A well-behaved nine-month-old poses politely.

CHAPTER 8

A collar with an ID tag attached is a must for your dog's training and safety.

dog to walk like a gentleman on your left side and to sit as you wait to cross the street. Recall is very important if your dog either escapes from the yard or breaks his leash and you need to call him back. Remember, it is essential to have an obedient and reliable Doberman.

Following is a short rundown of the commands. If you attend puppy classes or obedience training classes, you will have professional assistance in teaching these commands. However, you and your dog can learn these very basic exercises on your own.

Every Doberman must be trained to sit upon command. This is a basic exercise and will serve as the basis for other commands.

SIT

This is the exercise with which you should begin. Place your dog on your left side as you are standing and say "Sit" firmly. As you say this, run your hand down your dog's back and gently guide him into a sitting position. Praise him, hold him in this position for a few minutes, release your hand, praise him again and give him a treat. Repeat this several times a day, perhaps as many as ten times, and soon your pup will understand what you want.

Your Doberman must obey your commands not only in your backyard but also out in public among the distractions of people, activity, other dogs, etc.

STAY

Teach your dog to stay in a seated position until you call him. Have your dog sit and, as you say "Stay," place your hand in front of his nose and take a step or two, no more at the beginning, away. After ten seconds or so, call your dog. If he gets up before the end of the command, have him sit again and repeat the stay command. When he stays until called (remembering to start with a very short period of time), praise him and give him a treat. As he learns this command, increase the space that you move away from the dog as well as the length of time that he stays.

Teach your dog to sit by your left side before you begin walking together.

HEEL

Have your dog on your left side, with his leash on, and teach him to walk with you. If your pup lunges forward, give the leash a quick snap and say a firm "No." Then continue to walk your dog, praising him as he walks nicely by your side. Again, if he lunges, snap his leash quickly and say a smart "No." He will quickly learn that it is easier and more pleasant to walk by your side. Never allow him to lunge at someone passing by you.

DOWN

This will probably be the most complicated of the five basic commands to teach. Place your dog in the sit position, kneel down

Once your dog will sit reliably, you can begin teaching him to stay. Gradually increase your distance from him and the amount of time in which he is expected to stay.

next to him and place your right hand under his front legs and your left hand on his shoulders. As you say "Down," gently push his front legs out into the down position. Once you have him down, talk gently to him, stroke his back so that he will be comfortable and then praise him.

From the sit/stay, you and your Doberman can progress to the down/stay, using your hand as a "stop sign."

COME

Also known as the recall, this command is a vital lesson for all dogs and their owners. A positive approach to the come exercise is all that is necessary. You have to convince the young puppy that coming to his owner can only lead to happy, fun, positive experiences. Never, never, *never* call your dog to you to correct him. If you do, he will never obey because he is a smart Doberman—he knows when to run the

Start with the dog in position at your left side before stepping out in front of him to give the stay command.

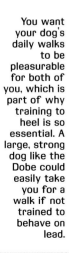
other way! Use the dog's name every time you call him to you. Put on a happy face and a happy voice so that he thinks coming to you is the best possible thing in the world. Give him a tasty treat every time he comes to you, and greet him with loving hugs and kisses. Who wouldn't want to run towards the kissy-face guy with a yummy snack? As long as you keep Come a fun command, your Doberman will respond in a positive way.

If you find that your Doberman is unresponsive to the come command (and your best smoked pork), you will have to resort to practicing the command on a 25-foot line. A little tug on the line and the puppy will get the idea that "Come"

You want your dog's daily walks to be pleasurable for both of you, which is part of why training to heel is so essential. A large, strong dog like the Dobe could easily take you for a walk if not trained to behave on lead.

Begin your Dobe's training with a light nylon or cotton lead. In time you will practice without the leash.

means "Come and get it!" Practice makes perfect, but don't overdo the treats or in six weeks you'll have a tubby puppy who is selective about when to hear your call and when to ignore it.

ADDITIONAL TIPS

With a Doberman, training is essential and it should be started at a very early age. A big part of training is patience, persistence and routine. Teach each command the same way every time, do not lose your patience with the dog, as he will not understand what you are doing, and reward him for performing his command properly. With a Doberman, you will find that your puppy will learn these commands very

CHAPTER 8

You want your Doberman to come running eagerly whenever he hears you call him.

quickly. Your friends, when they come to your house for a dinner party, will also appreciate a well-behaved dog who will not jump on their clothing or land in their laps while they are having cocktails..

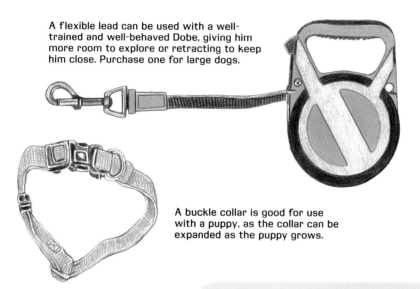

A flexible lead can be used with a well-trained and well-behaved Dobe, giving him more room to explore or retracting to keep him close. Purchase one for large dogs.

A buckle collar is good for use with a puppy, as the collar can be expanded as the puppy grows.

DOBERMAN PUPPY TRAINING

Overview

- Part of puppy training is socializing your pup to people, other dogs and new situations and surroundings.
- Puppy Kindergarten classes offer the advantages of professional guidance plus interaction with other puppies and owners.
- A positive, motivational method, utilizing treats and lots of praise, is the best way to train any dog.
- The basic commands are Sit, Down, Stay, Heel and Come.
- Commands are necessary for good manners and for your dog's safety.
- Keep training fun, positive and, most of all, consistent.

CHAPTER 9

Feeding Your Doberman Pinscher

Nutrition for your puppy is actually very easy. Dog-food companies hire many scientists and spend millions of dollars on research to determine what will be a healthy diet for your dog at each life stage. Your breeder should have been feeding a premium puppy food and you should continue on with the same variety. As the dog matures, you will change over to the adult variety of the same dog food brand. Do not add vitamins or anything else unless your vet suggests that you do so. Do not think that, by cooking up

Find out what the breeder was feeding to the pups. He should provide you with a diet sheet so that you can continue with the same food. Any changes should be made gradually.

a special diet, you will turn out a product that will be more nutritional than what the dog-food companies are providing.

Your young puppy will probably be fed three times a day and perhaps as many as four times a day. As he starts growing, you will cut his meals to two times a day, in the morning and in the evening. By the time he reaches eight months of age, you will be changing over to the adult-formula dog food. You can check your dog food's label for the amount, per pound of weight, that you should be feeding your dog. Your breeder is also an excellent source of advice.

There is no better food for a puppy than his mother's milk for the first weeks of life. Your puppy will be fully weaned and on a diet of solid food by the time he is old enough to come home with you.

To the dry kibble, you will add water to moisten it and possibly a tablespoon or so of a canned brand of dog food for flavor. Avoid giving your dog "people food," as this can cause stomach upset; some foods are even toxic to dogs. Give him a dog treat at

The Doberman will grow quickly. Some breeders suggest using elevated bowls for his food and water to aid his digestion. There is still debate about this practice.

CHAPTER 9

Mealtime is time to practice good manners. Your Doberman eats when you say it's time, so he should learn to wait politely until you give the OK.

bedtime. Keep a good covering of flesh over his ribs, but do not let your dog become a fat boy! However, the more active the dog, the more calories he will need. Always have fresh drinking water available. This may include a bowl of water in the kitchen and another outside in the yard. Change the water often and keep the bowl clean.

We've briefly mentioned bloat, a dangerous condition that can be prevented by taking precautions related to feeding. Never allowing your Doberman Pinscher adult or puppy to gulp food or water and restricting exercise for an hour before and at least two hours after meals are among the preventative measures. Discuss a complete plan of prevention with your vet.

A good chew is like an "after-dinner mint." Along with a diet of good dry food, chew toys help to keep the dog's teeth clean and breath fresh.

FEEDING YOUR DOBERMAN PINSCHER

Overview

- Feed your Doberman a top-quality dog food. This is the most reliable and convenient way to provide complete and balanced nutrition for your dog.
- Your breeder can advise you about the correct amount to feed your Dobe.
- Adhere to a feeding schedule throughout the dog's life. A puppy will eat three or four times daily; an adult only twice.
- Bloat is a life-threatening condition that affects deep-chested dogs. It is related to eating, feeding and exercise habits.
- Your Doberman's health relies upon a proper diet.

Home Care for Your Doberman

Every home with a pet should have a first-aid kit. You can acquire all of these items at one time, but more likely you will add them to your kit (oftentimes a box) as you need them. Many of these items can be purchased very reasonably from your local drug store. Here are the items you will need:

- Alcohol for cleaning a wound;
- Antibiotic salve for treating the wound;
- Over-the-counter eye wash in case your dog gets something in his eyes or just needs to have his eyes cleaned—"to get the red out";

Dogs need different types of care at different stages of life. One thing that remains constant is their need for owners who look after them well.

- Forceps for pulling out wood ticks, thorns and burrs;
- Styptic powder for when a toenail has been trimmed too short and bleeds;
- Rectal thermometer;
- A nylon stocking to be used as a muzzle if your pet should be badly injured.

You always want your Dobe to be able to run like the athlete he is. Buying from a breeder who screens his stock for dysplasia and other orthopedic disorders.

Now that your dog is mature and remaining well, he will only need a yearly visit to the veterinary clinic for a check-up and a booster shot for vaccines. At these visits, you may want to have the veterinarian scrape his teeth and express his anal glands.

You may purchase a dental tool and clean the teeth yourself to gently scrape away any tartar. Some animals will let you do this and others will not. Your Dobe may object less to a weekly toothbrushing, using a brush and paste made for dogs. A dog treat every night before bedtime will help

Your Doberman looks up to you for daily care and attention to his health. This is one of the responsibilities that you take on when you add a dog to your life.

to reduce tartar buildup.

Expressing the anal glands is not the greatest of tasks. Besides being quite smelly, you may find that it is just plain easier to have this done during the yearly trip to the vet's clinic. On occasion, the anal glands will become impacted; veterinary assistance will be required to empty them.

By now, you know your dog well, you know how much he eats and sleeps and how hard he plays. As with all of us, on occasion he may "go off his feed" or appear to be sick. If he has been nauseated for 24 to 36 hours, or had diarrhea for the same amount of time, or has drank excessive water for five or six days, a trip to the veterinarian is in order. Make your appointment and tell the receptionist why you need the appointment now.

The veterinarian will ask you the following questions:

• When did he last eat a normal meal? How long has he been disinterested in food?
• How long has he had diarrhea or been vomiting?
• Has he eaten anything in the last 24 hours?
• Could he have eaten a toy or a piece of clothing or anything else unusual?
• Is he drinking more water than usual?

The vet will check him over, take his temperature and pulse, listen to his heart, feel his stomach for any lumps, look at his gums and teeth for color and check his eyes and ears. He will probably also draw blood to run tests. At the end of the examination, he will decide how to treat the dog's illness. He may send your dog home with you with some antibiotics, take some x-rays or keep the dog overnight for observation. Follow your vet's instructions and you will find that, very often, your dog will be back to normal in a day or two. In the meantime, feed him light

Show your Doberman how much you love him by always maintaining him in top condition.

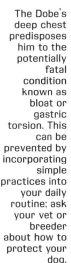

CHAPTER 10

meals and keep him quiet, perhaps confined to his crate.

Parasites can be a problem and there are certain ones of which you should be aware. Heartworm can be a deadly problem and dogs in some parts of the country are more vulnerable to this than others. Heartworms become very massive and wrap themselves around the dog's heart. If not treated, the dog will eventu-ally die. In the spring, call your veterinarian and ask if your dog should have a heartworm test. If so, take him to the clinic and he will be given a test to make certain that he is clear of heartworm. He then will be put on heartworm preven-tative medication. This is important, particularly if you live in areas where mosquitoes are present.

The Dobe's deep chest predisposes him to the potentially fatal condition known as bloat or gastric torsion. This can be prevented by incorporating simple practices into your daily routine; ask your vet or breeder about how to protect your dog.

Fleas are also a problem, but particularly in the warmer parts of the country. You can purchase flea powder or a flea collar from the pet shop or ask your veterinarian what he suggests that you use. If you suspect fleas, lie your dog on his side, use a flea comb on the coat and see if you find any skipping, jumping or skittering around of little bugs.

Ticks are more prevalent in areas where there a numerous trees. Ticks are small (to start) and dark, and they like to attach themselves to the warm parts of the ear, the leg pits, face folds, etc. The longer they are on the dog, the bigger they become, filling themselves with your pet's blood and becoming as big as a dime. Take your forceps and carefully pull the tick out to make sure you get the pincers. Promptly flush the tick down the toilet or light a match to it. Put alcohol on the wound and a dab of antibiotic salve. Let common sense and a good veterinarian be your guide in coping with these health problems.

HOME CARE FOR YOUR DOBERMAN

Overview

- Visit your local drug store and purchase the necessary items for a well-stocked doggie first-aid kit.
- Be vigilant about your dog's annual veterinary visits.
- Pay attention to your dog's dental care and anal-sac health in between trips to the vet.
- Know your dog so that you'll recognize when something is wrong.
- Get your dog to the vet right away if you suspect a problem. Be prepared to answer the vet's questions about your dog's daily routine and symptoms.
- Practice parasite control. Check your dog often, have him tested and use proper preventatives.

Grooming Your Doberman Pinscher

Do understand before purchasing your Doberman that he will need some grooming and attention to his hygiene. However, a big plus with this breed is that there is a very minimal amount of grooming required, unlike a Poodle or some other heavily coated breed.

A brush that has soft to medium bristles is recommended to keep your dog's coat looking shiny and clean. Usually, a weekly brushing will do the trick. A suitable bristle

Even the Dobe's short coat can hide bumps, fleas or other signs of irritation, so going over his skin and coat with your hands can help detect any abnormalities.

brush can be purchased from your local pet-supply store. A mitt that fits over your hand, smooth on one side and with soft wire pins on the other side, is excellent for the Doberman. A bath is certainly recommended when your dog is very dirty, but often a rubdown with a damp cloth will be ample for cleaning. Frequent bathing will deprive the dog's coat of important oils. In general, baths are recommended twice a year, in the spring and the fall.

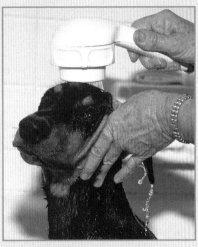

Part of a young Doberman's grooming is keeping his newly cropped ears clean and set correctly. Your vet and breeder will instruct you how to properly care for the ears.

It is important to trim your dog's toenails and it is best to start this within a week of bringing him home. Purchase a quality toenail trimmer made for dogs. You may want to purchase a styptic stick in case you trim the nail too short and cause it to bleed. There is a blood vessel called the "quick" that runs inside the nail. It is rather difficult to see in dark-nailed dogs and you may nick the blood vessel until you are more familiar with trimming the nails. If

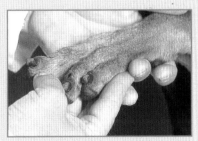

Be extra careful with clipping the Dobe's dark nails, as the "quick" vein in the nail is not visible. Only take off a little at a time.

Dobermans love the great outdoors, just like insects and parasites love dogs! Be attentive to keeping your dog pest-free and be sure no toxic plants are growing in areas where your dog spends time.

you do not start trimming the nails at a young age and accustoming your dog to the process, you will have a harder time with his pedicures as the dog becomes larger, heavier and more difficult to handle.

Once you establish a grooming routine with your Doberman you will find which tools you prefer to use.

If you give your dog hard biscuits to chew on, you will help to keep his teeth clean. You may also like to brush his teeth when you give his coat a weekly once-over. Also use this time to check that his ears are clean and healthy.

To wrap it up: This is a "wash and wear" dog. . .

easy to groom. Give him at least a weekly brushing, trim his toenails every month or so and wipe him down with a damp cloth when he looks like he needs it. Give him a bath only when it is necessary. You will now have a good-looking dog that you can be proud to be seen with!

GROOMING YOUR DOBERMAN PINSCHER

Overview

- Even though the Doberman is a low-maintenance dog, proper coat care is a vital part of his overall health-care program and must be initiated when the pup is young.
- The Doberman owner must tend to his dog's coat on a weekly basis. He should care for the dog's nails, ears and teeth as well.
- Only bathe your Doberman occasionally. In between baths, wiping down with a damp cloth will keep the coat clean.
- Be careful when trimming the dog's nails not to cut into the "quick." Have a styptic pencil on hand and give your pup treats and praise as you clip.

Keeping the Doberman Active

Many owners and their dogs are looking for challenging pursuits, and there are many activities to keep both of you very busy, active and interested. Dobermans can excel in many activities because of their intelligence, their willingness to please and their tenacity. After Puppy Kindergarten you may want to work toward the American Kennel Club Canine Good Citizen® award. This program, when successfully

Don't isolate your Dobe in the yard with nothing to do. This can lead to destructive behavior, separation anxiety and attempts to escape.

completed, shows that your dog will mind his manners at home, in public places and with other dogs. This class is available to all dogs (pure-bred or otherwise) of any age. It's a fun course and is useful for everyday life. There are ten steps, including accepting a friendly stranger, sitting politely for petting, accepting light grooming and examination from a stranger, walking on a loose lead, coming when called, responding calmly to another dog, responding to distractions, down on command and remaining calm when the owner is out of sight for three minutes. Upon successful completion, your Dobe will receive an AKC Canine Good Citizen® certificate.

With the young pup, you will find that they like to play games of tug with a hard rubber toy, a knotted-up rope or a very sturdy sock. All puppies like to chase balls and return them to their owners.

"What do you mean I'm not a retriever?" A Dobe's favorite activity is anything he can do with his owner, and games of fetch provide enjoyable interaction.

Puppies have no trouble keeping active. They get plenty of exercise by exploring and playing; youngsters should never be forced to exercise or be exercised too vigorously.

Obedience is a sport in which the Doberman can excel. Obedience trials are either held by themselves or in conjunction with an AKC dog show. There are different levels, starting with Novice, where, upon completion of three passing "legs," the dog will earn a Companion Dog (CD) title. The courses then progress in difficulty, with Open being at the second level. The dog earns a Companion Dog Excellent (CDX) upon completion of three successful Open legs. The next class is Utility, which includes off-lead work, silent hand signals and picking the right dumbbells from a group of dumbbells. Not many dogs reach this level and it is a major accomplishment for both owner and dog when a Utility Dog (UD) title is achieved.

Agility, started in England, is a relatively new yet popular sport in the United States and can be easily found at dog shows. Look for the large, noisy ring filled with competitors and dogs running the obstacle course and excited spectators watching at ringside, joining in with cheers.

Dogs are taught to run a course that includes hurdles, ladders, jumps and a variety of other obstacles. There are a number of degrees in agility, depending upon the obstacles that the dog is able to conquer. The AKC defines agility as "The enjoyment of bringing together communication, training, timing, accuracy and just plain fun in the ultimate game for you and your dog." Agility provides lots of challenging exercise for both dog and owner.

The ultimate in titles is the Versatile Companion Dog. This title recognizes

A well-trained Doberman is a fun companion to take along on all of your adventures.

CHAPTER 12

The ever-vigilant Doberman keeps watch over the home and yard as a valiant protector of his family and territory.

those dogs and handlers who have been successful in multiple dog sports. In order to excel at any of the foregoing activities, it is essential to belong to a dog club where there is equipment and facilities for practice. Find a good training school in your area and attend a class as a spectator before enrolling. If you like the facility, the instructor and the type of instruction, sign your dog up for the next series of lessons, which will probably be held two times a week with a choice of mornings or evenings.

Canine sports have become so popular with the public that there should be little difficulty in finding a training facility. You will find it a great experience, working with your dog and meeting new people with whom you will have a common interest. Your success will take time and interest on your part, and a willing dog working on the other end of the leash.

Schutzhund is another discipline that Dobermans can enjoy and excel at. Started in Germany for German Shepherds and other working breeds, it is a sport that demands the best out of your dog. Schutzhund-trained dogs are not attack dogs, as some think, but dogs that are trained for courage, intelligence and a sound temperament. When taking up this training with your dog, it is absolutely essential that you attend a reputable class with qualified trainers. There are many regional Schutzhund clubs all over the US. Contact the American Working Dog Federation (www.awdf.net) for more information about Dobes in Schutzhund.

Of course, the easiest way to keep your dog active and fit is to take him for a

Doberman Pinscher

A day by the lake and perhaps a swim? Your talented Doberman might enjoy diving in if you visit a safe body of water.

good walk every morning and evening. This will be good for you, too! Playing games with your dog will delight him. Chasing balls, catching Frisbees® or retrieving toys are always great fun for a dog. Dobermans have very strong jaws and teeth, so you need to purchase the best of rubber toys to have them last more than one or two play sessions. Never give your Dobe a toy or ball that is small enough for him to swallow. This could cause choking or an emergency trip to the vet to have the object removed.

Dobermans are working dogs and love to have work to do! With their intelligence and their willingness to learn quickly, they can be grand pets for you. Check out your local Doberman Pinscher club and you will find that the club holds many activities that you and your dog can enjoy. In addition, you will have the opportunity to meet other Doberman owners and exchange stories!

KEEPING THE DOBERMAN ACTIVE

Overview

- Once your pup has learned the basic commands, you can pursue the AKC's Canine Good Citizen® certificate with him.
- Keep your puppy active with games and gentle play, providing interesting activity that's not too strenuous for his growing frame.
- Obedience, agility and Schutzhund training are just three of the myriad aspects of the dog sport suitable for Dobermans and their owners.
- The best type of activity is that which dog and owner do together. Daily walks, retrieving games and including your Dobe in the family's activities whenever possible will keep him fit and mentally stimulated.

Your Doberman and His Vet

One of the first things to do when bringing home your dog is to find a good veterinarian. Your breeder, if from your area, should be able to recommend someone; otherwise, it will be your job to find a clinic that you like. Ask other dog owners whose opinions you trust to offer recommendations.

When selecting a veterinarian, it is always wise to find someone, for convenience, who is located near your home. Find a veterinarian that you like and trust, and be confident that he knows what he is

Your vet will help you care for your Dobe's ears, from post-cropping care to keeping them mite-free.

doing. Make sure he likes Dobes and knows how to treat a large dog. See that the office looks and smells clean. It is your right to check on fees before setting up an appointment and you will usually need an appointment. If you have a satisfactory visit, take the business card so that you have the clinic's number and the name of the veterinarian that you saw. Try and see the same vet each time, as he will personally know the history of your dog and your dog will be familiar with him.

Your chosen vet should have experience with the Dobe in particular, or at least large-breed dogs. Look at the breed's size at only four-and-a-half-months old!

Inquire if the clinic takes emergency calls and, if they do not, as many no longer do, get the name, address and telephone number of the emergency veterinary service in your area and keep this with your veterinarian's phone number. On your first visit, take along the health records that your breeder gave you, detailing the shots that your puppy has had, so that the veterinarian will know which

A breeder's first concern is that good health and genetic soundness are passed to each generation in every litter.

series of shots your pup should be getting. You should also take in a fecal sample for a worm test.

The recommended vaccines are for distemper, infectious canine hepatitis, parvovirus infection and parainfluenza. Although this seems like an impressive list of shots, there is one shot that will cover all of these viruses: DHLPP. This series of shots will start between six and ten weeks, which means that the breeder will be giving the first shots to the litter and your vet will have to finish up the series of three shots, given at four-week intervals.

The following are basic diseases for which vaccines are commonly given:

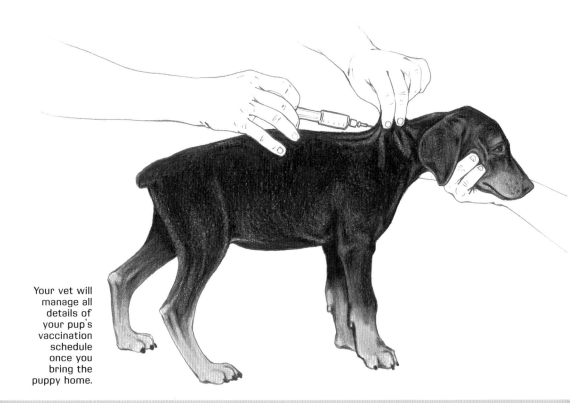

Your vet will manage all details of your pup's vaccination schedule once you bring the puppy home.

Every puppy in the litter from which you make your selection should be healthy and alert, ensuring that your pup has gotten the best start in life.

1. Distemper, at one time, was the scourge of dog breeding but with proper immunization and a clean puppy-rearing area, this no longer presents a problem to the reputable breeder.

2. Canine hepatitis, very rare in the United States, is a severe liver infection caused by a virus.

3. Leptospirosis is an uncommon disease that affects the kidneys and it is rare in puppies, occurring mostly in adult dogs.

4. Parvovirus is recognized by fever, vomiting and diarrhea. This is a deadly disease for pups and can spread very easily through their feces. The vaccine is highly effective in preventing the virus.

The Doberman is a relatively healthy dog, but there are some problems within the breed of which you should be aware.

Hip dysplasia is a major concern, as it is in most medium-sized and large

At your Doberman's physical exams, the vet will look into the ears for any signs of trouble. You should never probe into the ear yourself; always alert the vet if you suspect that something is wrong.

bone) fails to fit into the socket in the hip bone and there is not enough muscle mass to hold the joint together. This can often be a very painful problem for the dog, causing him to limp or to move about with great difficulty. Affected dogs must be managed by thera-peutic methods. In severe cases, there are surgical treatments that have proven effective. All Dobermans that are bred should have normal hips as determined by x-rays and approved by the Ortho-pedic Foundation for Animals (OFA).

Chronic active hepatitis (CAH) is an inflammatory condition that causes the liver to degenerate, with the final outcome being liver failure. This is a disease that is found in several other breeds but it is more prevalent in the Doberman. This disease can be treated in some dogs with cortico-steroids, but in one-third of

breeds. Hip dysplasia is an inherited disease in which the head of the femur (thigh

the cases there will be no treatment and death will be the outcome.

Dilated cardiomyopathy is a form of congestive heart failure, a disease of the heart in which the heart muscle becomes dysfunctional over time. There are eight breeds, of which the Doberman is one, in which 90% of the cases are seen. Onset in Dobermans, where it has been studied extensively, is usually between two and five years, and then the disease progresses insidiously over the next several years. The illness, if diagnosed at an early stage, which often it is not, can sometimes be controlled by medication. However, the long-term prognosis is not good.

Von Willebrand's disease (VWD) is a blood-clotting disorder similar to hemophilia except in dogs it will affect both sexes. If the dog has the disease and is injured or has surgery, it may bleed more than a dog without the disease. If the

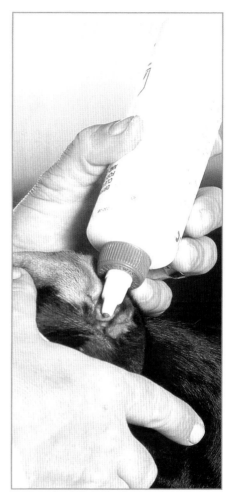

Your vet may need to administer medication if there is an ear infection, mite infestation or other problem.

disease is severe, there may be spontaneous bleeding from the nose, mouth or bladder. Dogs are tested by a blood sample. Dogs with VWD should not be bred, as it is a hereditary disease.

Hypothyroidism is an autoimmune disorder of the thyroid gland. Diagnosis can

A Doberman's good health will shine through in his alert nature, clean eyes and shiny coat.

be made by a blood test and medication can be given for thyroid supplementation. This is a fairly treatable

disorder; many affected dogs live normal lives.

The Doberman can also have some eye and skin problems as well as cancer. Blue Dobermans may exhibit color dilution alopecia, which is a hereditary disease that the breeder can tell you about. The Doberman breed does have its share of health problems; however, the Doberman Pinscher Club of America is continually testing Dobermans and working on health research projects to try and eliminate many of these problems from breeding programs. You should be aware of these problems within the breed and ask the breeder if he has had his dogs tested. If he has, ask to see the certificates from the appropriate registries and do not just accept his word that the sire and dam of the litter have been tested for the various problems. This list may seem daunting, but

responsible breeders will have had their stock tested and will be doing their best to eliminate these problems in the breed.

Health guarantees are important and a responsible breeder will give you a contract that will guarantee your pup against certain congenital defects. This guarantee will be limited in time to six months or one year. If there is a problem within this time, he will possibly replace the pup or offer some refund of the purchase price.

A last note: You should consider neutering or spaying your Doberman; the breeder may require this for pups not destined for showing or breeding. A neutered male will be less aggressive, less apt to lift his leg in the house and have less of a tendency to mount. A neutered female will not come into season every six months. Neutering has many health benefits, preventing or reducing the risk of various cancers and other serious problems.

YOUR DOBERMAN AND HIS VET

Overview

- Find a good vet in your area. Take recommendations from your breeder or other dog owners, and make sure you are comfortable with his personality, facility and fees, and confident about his skills.
- Bring along your pup's health records to your first visit and keep scheduled appointments for vaccinations and check-ups.
- The most common vaccination is the DHLPP combination shot.
- Be aware of the breed-specific health concerns and ask your breeder to see relevant health clearances on the parents of your pup. A good breeder will give a health guarantee.
- Spaying or neutering offers many advantages to the pet-only dog.

CHAPTER 14

The Aging Doberman Pinscher

As your dog starts aging, he will start to slow down. He will not play as hard or as long as he used to and he will sleep more. He will find the sunbeam in the morning hours and take a long nap. At this time, you will probably put him on a senior dog food, but do continue to watch his weight, as it is more important than ever not to let your Doberman become obese in his senior years. You will notice that his muzzle will become gray, and you may see a opacites in his eyes, signs

Dobermans remain active parts of their owners' lives, no matter their age.

of cataracts. And as he becomes older, he may become arthritic.

Continue your walks, making them shorter, and give him a baby aspirin when he appears to be stiff. Keep up with your grooming, as both you and he will like to have him look and smell clean. Watch for lumps and bumps and take him to the veterinarian if you are concerned. Incontinence can also become a problem with the older dog. This is frustrating for you and hard on the house, but he hasn't become "unhousebroken"; rather, his muscle control is fading.

The Doberman is a hardy breed that stays alert into the senior years.

Veterinary care has improved much over the last decade or two, as has medical care for humans. Your veterinarian can now do much to extend your dog's life if you want to spend the money. While this will extend his life, it will not bring back his youth. Your primary concern should be to help your animal live out his life comfortably, and there are

A well-trained Doberman is a joy for his whole life. Make your senior feel useful by continuing to practice his commands.

medications that can be helpful for this goal. Whatever you decide, try to put your dog's well-being

Watch your dog's weight as he gets older. Less activity means more chance of weight gain, which can compromise a senior's overall health.

and comfort ahead of your emotions and do what will be best for your pet.

When the end inevitably comes, always remember the many wonderful years that your pet gave to you and your family. With that thought, it may not be long before you are looking for a new puppy for the household. And there you are, back at the beginning with a cute bundle of joy, ready for another ten years or more of happiness!

THE AGING DOBERMAN PINSCHER

Overview

- Your older dog's activity level will decrease as he ages.
- Keep an eye on your senior dog's diet and weight, as obesity is especially harmful to older dogs.
- Graying, eye problems and arthritis are common in senior dogs.
- Keep up with your Doberman's regular routines, making allowances for the changes that accompany aging.
- Give your senior Doberman the best veterinary care that you can, as well as the good care and affection you've shown him all his life.